UPDOG

US MILITARY BRANCHES

THE US ARMY IN ACTION

Percy Leed

Lerner Publications ◆ Minneapolis

Lerner Publications Company
An imprint of Lerner Publishing Group, Inc.
241 First Avenue North
Minneapolis, MN 55401 USA

For reading levels and more information, look up this title at www.lernerbooks.com.

Main body text set in ITC Franklin Gothic Std.
Typeface provided by Adobe Systems.

Editor: Brianna Kaiser **Designer**: Mary Ross **Photo Editor:** Cynthia Zemlicka
Lerner team: Sue Marquis

Library of Congress Cataloging-in-Publication Data

Names: Leed, Percy, 1968– author.
Title: The US Army in action / Percy Leed.
Description: Minneapolis : Lerner Publications , [2023] | Series: US military branches (UpDog books) | Includes bibliographical references and index. | Audience: Ages 8–11 | Audience: Grades 2–3 | Summary: "The army's mission is to keep the US safe. Discover the history of the Army, the different jobs soldiers do, and the technology and equipment they use"— Provided by publisher.
Identifiers: LCCN 2021035566 | ISBN 9781728458267 (library binding) | ISBN 9781728463575 (lpaperback) | ISBN 9781728462493 (ebook)
Subjects: LCSH: United States. Army—Juvenile literature.
Classification: LCC UA25 .L44 2023 | DDC 355.00973—dc23

LC record available at https://lccn.loc.gov/2021035566

Manufactured in the United States of America
1-50855-50192-11/10/2021

TABLE OF CONTENTS

MEET THE ARMY

Wildfires burn forests. Firefighters need help.

The army can help during natural disasters.

NATURAL DISASTER:
an event, such as a fire or flood, that could hurt many people

The army's goal is to keep the US safe. It started during the Revolutionary War (1775–1783).

The army has many troops. Over eight hundred thousand soldiers are in the army.

TROOP:
a group of soldiers

Army engineers build and maintain water systems such as dams.

ENGINEER: a person who designs and builds things

They also study drones and other technology.

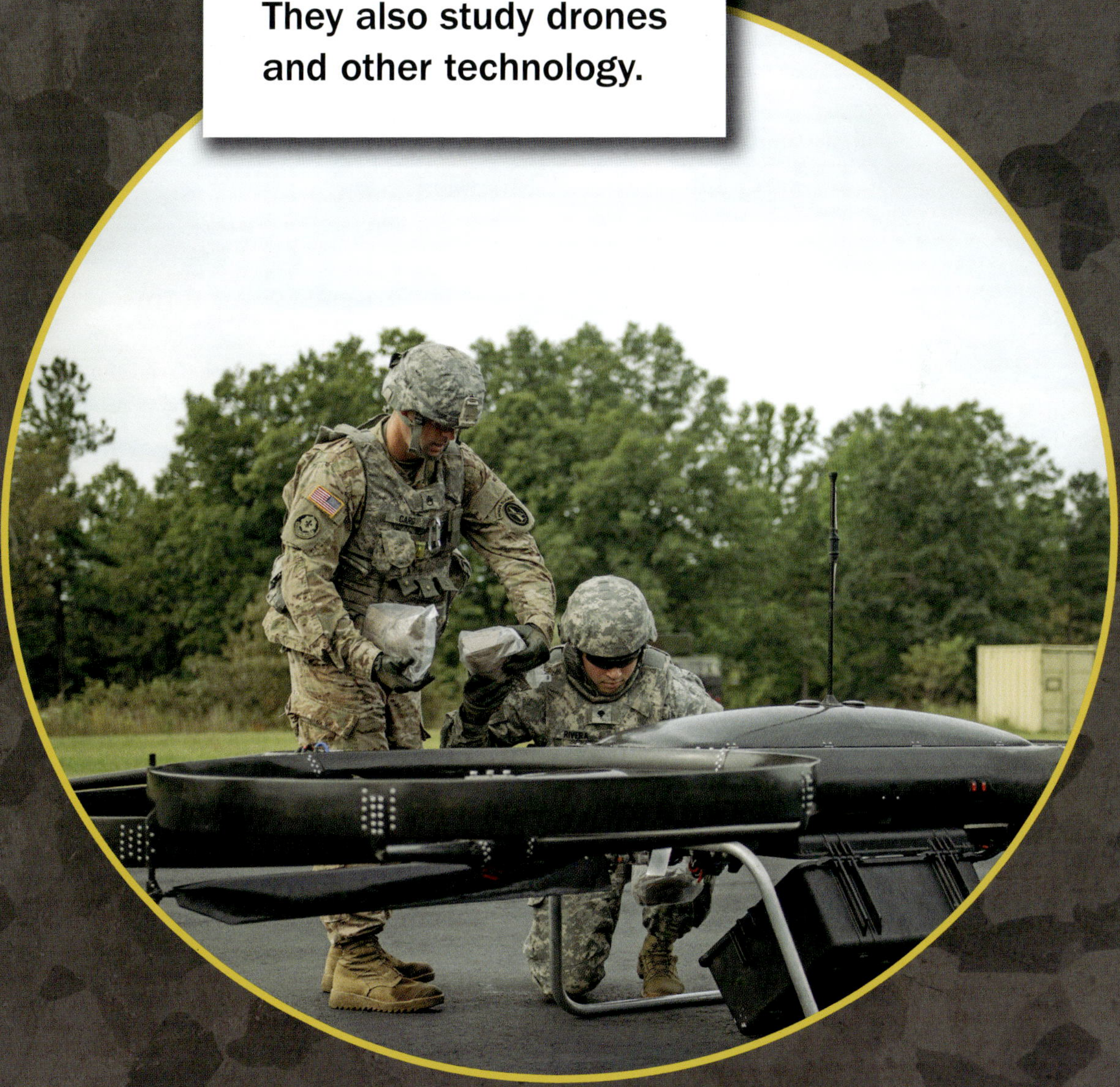

TECHNOLOGY: the use of science to do practical things

The medical team stops the spread of diseases in the US and in other places.

They also keep the soldiers healthy.

VEHICLE CLOSE-UP

With scientists, the army built the PackBot. It safely gets rid of dangerous things, such as bombs.

UP NEXT!

ARMY ROBOTS

The army uses robots for jobs that are too dangerous for a person to do.

It works with scientists at colleges to improve the robots.

It also tests new robots.

The army is working on robots with legs.

UP NEXT!

ACTIVE AND RESERVE

The army has two parts: active and reserve. Active members are currently working.

Reserve members train and are ready to help if needed.

The army works all over the world. It's one of the biggest military groups.

MILITARY MISSION

AN ARMY TROOP SEES A BOMB. WHAT SHOULD THEY DO?

A. Get rid of it themselves

B. Have a robot remove it

C. Have someone else look at it

Answer: B

GLOSSARY

engineer: a person who designs and builds things

natural disaster: an event, such as a fire or flood, that could hurt many people

technology: the use of science to do practical things

troop: a group of soldiers

CHECK IT OUT!

Army
https://kids.britannica.com/kids/article/army/352785

Billings, Tanner. *The U.S. Army*. New York: Rosen, 2022.

Hustad, Douglas. *US Army Equipment and Vehicles*. Minneapolis: Abdo, 2021.

Military Engineering Facts for Kids
https://kids.kiddle.co/Military_engineering

Morey, Allan. *U.S. Army*. Minneapolis: Jump!, 2021.

United States Armed Forces
https://www.ducksters.com/history/us_government/united_states_armed_forces.php

INDEX

PHOTO ACKNOWLEDGMENTS

Image credits: Sgt. 1st Class Jimmy Norris/US Army, p. 4; Sgt. 1st Class Donna Davis/US Army, p. 5; Sgt. Raquel Birk/US Army, p. 6; Spc. Tin P. Vuong/US Army, p. 7; Trevor Welsh/US Army, p. 8; Pvt. Gabriel Silva/ US Army, p. 9; Jason W. Edwards/US Army, p. 10–¬¬11; U.S. Army Photo, pp. 13, 20; Spc. Ryan Lucas/US Army, p. 14; Terrance Bell/US Army, p. 15; Master Sgt. Jeffrey Duran/US Army, p. 16; Jeffrey Greenberg/Universal Images Group/Getty Images, p. 17; Staff Sgt. Jae Jung/US Army, p. 18; 1st Lt. Stephanie Snyder/US Army, p. 19. Design elements: Andrey_Kuzmin/Shutterstock.com, anyababii/Getty Images.

Cover: Cpl. Geordan J. Tyquiengco/US Army.